BRAIN'S NATURAL LENS

LOVE IS THE LEADER

KUMAR ABHISHEK

I dedicate this book to all the poets of our country India specially the women poets who have to inspire the world with their verses and rhymes and at the same time capture the time for the family and loved ones.I think poetry is the thinking of developed MINDS. And who are more matured than women whom gravity balances the society and I think the era of womenhood has come.My heart goes out to the male poets who took the time to let the society and people grow, function and mentally more balancing the world.I agin like to repeat that "Poetry Is The Thinking Of Developed Mind".

I dedicate this book to all the poets of our country especially

the women poets who have [illegible] the world [illegible]

and rhymes and at the same time [illegible]

and loved one I think poetry is the [illegible]

And who are more mature than [illegible] whom [illegible]

[illegible]

[illegible]

[illegible]

[illegible]

Contents

Contents

Preface

WHEN I THINK OF WRITING A PREFACE THE FIRST THING THAT COMES IN MY MIND IS LOVE.The most Crystal Kind of formal or informal thing in this world is love.Love is kindness not condition, but people often misguided or due to the thirst fall into the prey of mirage developed between kindness and condition.One more reason of formation of mirage is kindness of so many kind.This creates a lot of assertion. Love has no boundaries. Love between love birds is the purest form of love. Love between brothers and sisters is the love like water droplet on a peepul tree leaf. Love between Guru and disciple is like giver and beggar, one can never payback to a true guru. The most valuable and real form of love is between father and son. A father is the director of his child and directs the unwind light unto colors.He teaches you to love the human race. He teaches you that service to human kind is crystal Kind. Mother, Maa, Mom, Mumy, Amma, say it by any name the calling may not be parallel but the meaning and love is unparalleled.Mother gives you wings to fly.She is the first beloved, first brother and sister, first guru, and the first father.Actually mother is the Crystal of life and she is the kindest person for the child.Thats why I wish to write the preface about love which is crystal Kind.She love unconditionally, but never expect a kind word from her child.She gives you the vision of life. She introduce you to the world.A father directs you to love him or her, but a mother inherits love in you.Yes Mother is the crystal form of Love.

1. Waves Pegs!

Old love ardent warm orientation,
Rolling seashore roaming air,
Land of chords of row mass is the happiness indeed,
God of magenta alarms words amass grips,
Child mind is the territory of Lords dark shadow,
Good vibes of nine O'clock remain the witness,
Of the deep vanished creator,
Love vivid and words vintage,
Krystal kind of ships pearls poem,
Mood of the docks in the sea borrow air,
Hiccups of the water bubble in the krystal of hiding waves pegs!
Heaven blood shiver in the waves humankind whole hurled,
Deal of the vandalised hours should have wired fruits, wish of supposed ships,
Heaven blood shivered yet to be honoured warmth vanishing the power of insights,
Pained owl and crowded crows of ashes of pheonix started to paint shadow,
Seeds of plants, dwelling of the hoarded world of ships,
Swords of idol Lord waranty the true-ship,
Death is sure after getting old in the wisdom of world without happy gossip of angels, "Long live the flexibility,
Looking at the molten distance from the eyes of worried sky, " Love is scaler not the vector", whispered the clouds,
Barbarism stops at the wish of the pearl drops from sky ship!

2. Heart Beats Offer Magical

Heart beats offer magical,
In front of God, no formality, don't be formal,
Anything in the beginning needs balance,
Once the balance achieved concurrence,
We human being, nature or the Universe has to be course critical,
Nothing is fixed in the world,
Nothing is formal if you seriously see the whole hurled,
Eye can't see it's solution but
Solution,
But those who think of problem or question
Are the one who thrive this world based on attraction,
Attraction could be varying sometimes it is called gravitational reaction,
Sometimes it is called desire,
Sometimes, an invisible wire,
No one has reached the final conduction,
Are subject to many unknown perfection,
Here everybody is trapped between birth and death,
We are only living on a suspended earth,
Suspension because of negative perfection,
This negative perfection is time and space, infinite but accessable only fraction.

3. Cars like Stars

The vanished stars,
Had once raised the bars,
The night's moving cars
On the street of sky from Mars;

The moons are bike,
The best is bicycle like;
The astroid destroyed part of sun psych,
The 'ether' is the fuel subject to price hike;

This whole thing has a logo,
Which creates the people's choice, go,
Solar system is bus, train and cargo,
Planes and satellites are galaxies with ego.

4. Pattern

Have you ever thought?
Why are birds all about?
What they think about human being?
What is the link sought their wing?

Have you ever thought?
Why human had never wings, never free, let them cought?
Like birds and many insects including butterfly,
Their flying wet wings sounds ...furrrr... to get dry,

Have you ever thought?
If human had got wings who would live on land & boat?
Why birds ever make their nest on trees and not on land surface?
Even they might got remotest corner on earth's base.

5. Laugh Out Dear

Laugh out dear, fully,
Laughter is an alternate of loss
Laugh out dear, regularly,
Laughter is the blooming of rose,

Laugh out dear, surely,
Laughter is the song of happiness,
Laugh out dear, very lively,
Laughter is free without taxes,

Laugh out dear, daily,
Laughter is life full of pranks,
Laugh out dear, so innocently,
Laughter is promotion of smiling thanks,

Lough out dear, timely,
Laughter is worth if there is good timing,
Laugh out dear, actually,
I know, I am embarrassing.

Laugh out dear, loudly,
Laughter is unique action,
Laugh out dear, frankly,
I may laugh, Newton's has done hard work on action & reaction.

6. Soul is Immortal

Soul is immortal,
It has wings immortal for flying,
And slowly swings in a zigzag manner,
Soul are the habit of human being,
As it is cordial and calculated incidence,
Which is clocked mostly as co-incidence,
This incidence is the difference ,
Between alive and alive soul,
Where human body a mere fence,
After life is a silence and invisibility,
It does not mean the soul is not alive,
Soul never rest in peace but peace rest in soul,
But human being is to be human in fence with common sense thrive.

7. Future Due

The world has an instinct,
To go beyond every hint,
Because any hint not enough,
To mark that suffering which makes us tough,
If the east has intrinsic value,
Then the west has every shade of blue,
If the glory of the east can defy sky,
Then the west can trigger higher than high.
Both is equally important and one in space view,
It is the matter of marching crew for-- past few, present hue&future due.

8. Crafted

To everything that welcome me in stages of my life,
To everyone who help me to win,
The time that let me heal in its course,
The friends who let me understand the rules of world convene,
The guardians who prefer to provide me all sort of happiness,
The strangers who gave me lessons of life,
The professionals who allow me to think beyond ,
The human nature that let me understand the resolution to all strife,

A big thank you to all these life pearls that comes like wave regularly and let my life crafted.

9. Life Is One

Life is one,
Make it fun,
Sadness undone,
Quality run,
Quantity in many ton,
Hurt non,
Loose gun,
Youth should learn,
Crime is to shun,
The earth spun,
Around the sun,
Time immemorial million,
Had won morn,.
Dews on flowers turn,
Sprinkled in crops of bun,
Who?I think the moon.

10. Delhi, The Heart Of India

Delhi, irrespective of political party's rule, the heart of India,
Yeah, the heart, the most tragic and magic idea,
Delhi, the lamp of pleasure light,
Is the cream extracted from all political fight,
From Lal Qila to Jama Masjid,
From Qutub Minar to India gate amid,
Delhi is the capital of india from long,
It deserve to be... It has secular tester tongue,
Question arises if it had all rounded financial circumference,
The answer lies in the Parliament the political heaven as Delhi's-dummy fence.

11. Bhagat Singh; Intensely Inspiring

When I thought of writing something about bhagat singh,
I suppose to find him a preamble of a fighter true son of the soil --his upbringing,
Life is shorter then our thinking,
It consist of flesh and bone together linking,
Bhagat singh sacrificed his life because he was twinkling,
In the sky of hope, freedom, patriotism, bringing a true morning,
A person who has tributed his life quest to be heard his singing,
There was no social media, news network, but yet his greatness transpired with wings,
Imagine how competent was his life yet he chose to end his life swinging,
He had contributed fire to patriotism &inspired how to live with pride, wisdom like a true king.

12. Capture some space

Capture some space,
Capture to impress,
Find the impression of working hands,
Impression is the mark of magic wands,
It is a start to pave the path of reconciliation,
A journey to discover truth of fraction,
I again reiterate capture some space,
Capture to impress,
God knows all the future,
His impressions are all over,
Trace his impression of foots,
He is here, he is there, the roots,
Capture some space, capture to impress.

13. Way Of Worship

I don't believe in the God;
Who want me to worship,
I don't believe in the God;
Who force me to believe idolship,
I don't believe in the God;
Who have done nothing for the poor outside his home(temple, church or mosque etc.)
I don't believe in the God;
Who reside in the heart of rich people as norm,
I don't believe in the God;
Who don't accept the erroneous pray of poor,
I don't believe in the God;
Who don't forgive mistakes residing in the narrow mind of people impure.

14. Pain Is Our Companion...

My price of work,
Is a chunk of torque,
It is simple,
But still a sample,
I want to convey,
How to intreprete my way,
Don't think too much,
Believe in karma's search,
Don't feel for result,
Don't feel for special cult,
I feel work as hot as soul,
I feel work as cool as ice berg in poles,
My commitment is about,
To the thing however it maybe only about,
Inititially I fought,
A war I had adjust a bout,
Within, may be people calling it depression,
But in my thought it is thought process realization.
Never scared of failure,
I remember a Hindi song sure,
"Rahi manva dukh ki chinta kyun satati hai,
Dukh toh apna sathi hai,"
(Nomad thinking why worried of pain,
Pain is our companion).

15. Now

When you look at India today,
What would inspire you,
Is the fact that it is young,
Which is like dynamite and new,

When you look at India today,
The life of our economy is young,
The whole scenario depend on self creation,
India's taste is not just today but now like tongue,

When you look at India today,
The lifestyle of youth must energise,
As well as being patient like old,
And make children to dream to become wise!

16. Honestly Trying For Change

Honestly trying for change,
Like words are dieing strange;
In the absence of grammar,
Killed due to reference armour,
But what happened to its beginning,
Is it alone or have friends like similar meaning,
I am writing according to my style,
Completing so many file,
The time has capacity to travel to a range,
Honestly trying for change,
That consist of compassion for other language,
But english a dominator,
It never bow it's head, even in front of its creator,
But could be inclined emotionally with its friends like french or spanish or italian,
But English fall for self love in any indigenous version,
A perfect friend at relax and professional at work to arrange,
Bringing honesty, and always honestly trying for change.

17. Life Here Is A Goose Bump

The world is temporarily,
A station to all of us,
But nothing is permanent,
Neither sun nor earth, nor the universe,
One day every layer will be finished,
Including the sun, which is young,
Will be older once it is done,
Then what would be needed to be done before bang?
What is the soul purpose of universe?,
Sometimes I feel earth is a sensor,
Life here is a goose bump,
By seeing its own miracle shadow everywhere.

18. Thethen

Thethen the world was filled with strangers,
Everyone was stranger & not engaged;
In the social media, there complete vacuum,
To one another thing are managed,
Only by seeing each other,
There were people who take notice of lonely lives called God's messenger,
Suddenly I waked up...
And realises,
Everything was dream,
& The vacuum of dream,
I thanked God,
It was only a dream,
Next was, I communicated,
In my surrounding,
I felt presence of...
All the well wishers,
Now I felt it was much needed dream,
As we are progressive,
From social to social media,
And from social media to being social,
The whole cycle completes,
Reminding me of a urdu saying;
Mia ki doud masjid tak.

19. Autumn Again

Autumn is in full thrive;
To take the evenings dive,
Autumn starts to shine in the sky,
Autumn is pride of the trees so high,
Pride because autumn leaves leave the tree,
After a ego clash setting separation to free,
Autumn this time with a plea,
To welcome winter with innate glee,
Autumn this time is in fear,
Of not coming again the autumn leaves very dear,
Autumn this time is real,
Saying an appeal,
Why God pain by pluck leaves when he has to heal?,
Its eternal method to repeal.

20. A Treat To Observe

Have you noticed?
The world is mixed,
to the people,
By the God eventual,
A treat to observe,
The God above,
Handling people's move,
With a attached woolen string,
In the form of Sun rays feeling,
Warming in a innate journey,
Of the earth, in turning any...
Bring here everything,
With infinite balancing...
Unity in diversity only,
Making human like God, strongly...

21. Crawling On The Smartphones

Hands engaged in smartphones,
Fingers crawling on the smartphones,
Like bacteria &ameoba to capture the zones,
My Hands up to let the bacteria to be fully grown's,
Looking to who is hunting these bacteria world wide Web runs.

22. RISEN THE PACE, BEGUN THE RACE

Every revolution starts from a baby step,
That first step is not less than Armstrong's leap,
After that everything become as usual,
Likewise our first step against all the odds are visual,
In the information and technology our first step was not a small leap,
But not less than men's first step in moon when compared deep,
After all it has renamed several times and now called digital India,
RISEN THE PACE, BEGUN THE RACE,
As we won against all odds against foreign invasions, atrocities etc, always,
But we fought and never gave up and the result was Newly Born IT Programme With Grace In The Face.

23. Unity Is Strength

The government has a different attitude towards south India,
The government is thinking or pretend north India's vision is super idea,
The govt. itself trying to prove that,
The people from South India are educated but...
Very simple and sophisticated and could not cop when hard times,
Where there is a need of gray shade, they will misstimes
And when there is a need of hard politics and tough measures they get fail,
The biggest mistake of this govt. is they want to project it tooth & nail,
That in North india the don't have any integrity,
And people of north India are united against southern part of the nation unity,
Simple people even get misguided of the different language, and culture,
I strongly reject this kind of discrimination, immature,
And want to convey that the govt. thinking wrong that they are so being carried away, in such invasion,
Today along with me the whole north India stand for solidarity with south India against discrimination.

24. What is missing in monsoon?

What is missing in monsoon?
We are missing vikram on the moon,
We are getting high fine(chalan) in mid market noon,
We are missing some great leader in the time to come.
Some leaders who were the legends and for India, a boon,
In monsoon we are missing monsoon at some places from June,
And heavy rainfall in some places on every dawn,
Nature has transmogrified into all in one;
Growing without restriction on and on,
The monsoon has ring the bell for the coming of autumn,
Don't you feel the pace of time, this year will end soon.

25. Social Order

Preamble of democracy is common men/women,
The direction it acquires is definite & towards people's proven,
Government is the radar-reader who decides it's life like pre-curser,
It is govt. who makes authority, higher the authenticity, higher it apply honesty to its power,
Politics is a Bullock cart whose bulls are freedom and fearlessness,
Politician are the driver of these bullock-cart Promises of destiny atleast before election nears,
Constitution is the benchmark of light & vision in every dark corner of the society,
In all, inclusiveness of opposition decides the authority of the government on duty.

26. God Is Guide

World wide,
Strong stride,
Life in pride,
Of beautiful side,
God is guide,
But why hide,
Like he abide,
Between the tide,
Freedom, the bride,
Of my I.d,
Who never lied,
Like the god who cried,
For the sky dried,
Finally he tried,
But failed and aside,
His bike ride,
Fortune never died,
Come again to hide,
Jocker fried,
My brain inside,
But I woke up before suicide,
And temporarily coincide,
Life win and enjoyed,
Everything else to avoid,
For the people annoyed,

Of the new dawn overjoyed,
Finding peace in the glide,
Blanket sky like an allied.

27. Mother; Without Any Option

Its raining endlessly,
Its paining endlessly,
Rain on the pain carelessly,
But who cares more than anybody selflessly,
"Mother" the true angel,
Never complain for any thing to deal,
"Mother" the tears of my eyes,
Never drop any wish always winner in her eyes,
"Mother" giving winners prize,
Always consider to give hero's prize,
"Mother" think about us as supreme,
However bad her child may be...
"Mother" always see child as the prince or princess like a royal dream,
However ordinary the child may be...
"Mother" is everything, child her pride,
She knows what is in the heart of child to guide,
"Mother" the only one assures everything done;
Like super-mom of the home,
"Mother" born and brought by till we could handle the life's run,
Leave us without taking CREDIT when old she become!

28. Cluster Of Coincidences

Coincidence made up of coincidentia(a latin word) and the coincide(An english word),

I think cluster of coincidences subject to truth,

Coincidences is happening thing,

It is a phenomenon by which one could draw attention for materialising to object,

Coincidence is like a bridge of a rope upon which people had to walk simultaneously,

It is like lightening by the random clouds all around,

Or anything which tends to accident, but not, is coincidence,

Coincidence social impact is that it had been made but never break,

It is a constructive design of the Almighty or His attacking approach to the substantial world.

29. Rainfall

Rainfall and thunderstorms,
Hit the city and all norms,
Finding the grass wet and in front of homes,
The loose soil has been the alarms of worms,
Same form the cocoon zooms;
The butterfly forms,
Raining the day and night comes,
With a challenge to wanderers who roams,
One day I was roaming,
In the village,
Rain druming,
Rain was gaming,
The game of racing,
Whenever I was stoping,
In the shade for hiding,
Rain stopped, irritating;
I restarted, the rain repeating,
This happened not once twice,
But five times,
So me fuming,
What I should be saying,
Nature's magic,
Or my timing,
All my understanding,
Drawn the conclusion,

It was amusing, assuming,
Or imitating.

30. Earth Model

What happened to people when they die,
Is a question asked to many scholar,
But they could only say date of expiry in archive,
A poet could discover many things in advance during writing,
There had been poet saying about death and live,
With different and difference in view & opinion respectively,
I believe their are co-ordinates where people travel and dive,
They just change the graph simultaneously,
Without realising,
Change of graph from one to other is like the world is standstill and alive,
And at the same time in motion with speed more than light,
The reality is in motion and standstill like divine,
Like the earth which is in motion, and we still think we are standstill.

31. Assembling The Country

Long ago a rusted shackle had tied an old civilization,
A civilization that had universal acceptance but a tired nation,
Tired of invasions, rulers, and fanaticism applied by the rulers,
By the time civilization absorbed and extracted every colors,
The new emerged, secular, established nation was named "Insteel",
Insteel got Independence and started a journey by breaking old shackle,
But when the shackles broke it had broken the part of the country with it,
Everything was shattered had got the hit,
Insteel was rusted, broken but ready to thrive in life and light,
There were heroes of liberation who were always ready to fight;
To fight with problems like poverty, injustice, old traditions, nil development and a innate darkness,
Nothing to reflect to showcase, but drops for "assembling a country", a new race,
To become an ocean of assembled hopes and thrust to achieve height,
And reborn as a country of fulfillment of everyone with pride and insight,
There were challenges but the infatuation of the heroes of freedom to course correct was limitless,
The stream of assembling a country was repelling every obstruction that come in its way and to face,
Even small child was contributing his capacity to impress,
A new dream of new Insteel came to face the reality and assess,

A new journey had started, but alas!With a separation of one state,
Like a character had been separated from a novel to a new fate,
Pain and separation had engulfed the whole insteel and the parted state,
But that was the destiny said one of the great freedom fighter in suffering act,
Time passed, the wound saturated and both state parted to their ways,
Insteel was not filled of anger of foreign invasion but looking for option to want of arrays,
There was a different unfulfillment in the Insteel that could be resulted in breakdown and revolt,
But the freedom fighters made the garland of problems for Insteel to suit,
All the disarray and all the disorder vanished and strong one Insteel evolved from the ashes,
Moderation was become their tool of running the nation forward in graces,
That formed a political arena as a backbone to fight the stress build up due to years of hardships,
That followed Insteel with different cruelty and unfaithfulness of far and near creeps,
The yearning was shaking but prevailing force to build a nation thrive at the right time,
And one of the great leader among them became the head of the nation to become "Prime",
The Prime was full of faith and united the whole Insteel into one,
To fetch new life, new methods into the Insteel bone,
He formed group of ministers to deal with every alarming problem in detail,

The "Prime" distributed the responsibility to make separate Constitution, that prevail,
And Insteel got a separate constitution to practice sail,
The constitution makers count every sense that dwell,
They found all colours of pearls in the deep organic ocean unbound,
Constitution of Insteel had to counter the length of mind from zero to social boundaries and stalling sound,
The lawmaker of Insteel insured that justice to all would be the theme,
And amount to connect the last person who remained torch bearer of the new flame,
The preface of the law was made on the basis of certainty, practicality and captivity of the people of Insteel,
Law were law and based on a frame that could suit it in a long run and apeal,
They confirmed the law put some effect to people while people should not effect the law,
The constitution was measuring the totality of Insteel's backwardness in the flow,
In every clause of the constitution were the merging of every section of the society to come on the surface;
To ensure social security, to curb poverty became the major directive in a moderate pace,
There was a need of guidance which could provide equality and rectify Inequality,
And a country where it was hard to define the uncertainty,
People crosses limits and hard to cascade law to cast,
The metal thus formed was hard to imply and apply and advocated in a stream vast,
All the lawmakers of the Insteel applied the constitution in a zeal,

As truth propagate in any condition, do not need excuse to deal,
Insteel started to run in a double pace of development in all direction,
With effective leadership of Prime Insteel then had its own democracy and constitution,
New ways were made and new doors of advancement started the new age of machinery and technique,
Insteel unfolded all its cards to compete with the then world's mystique,
But there were old traditions that had bounded the nation,
In which untouchability was the most alarming problem the country had faced as the institution,
Some problems like legal rights of women were among major problem that was needed to be shorted out,
So the Prime revolutionized a set of reforms and justice was brought,
He had stood for a fountain of education in the country,
And assure school and colleges, technical institutions, medical colleges, management institutes were the next entree,
Prime brought industrial set ups to employ the youth,
And mining, electricity, aviation, shipping etc were started in the story of growth,
Farmers than free from the bonded labour of zamindar,
And had their own rule on land to production at the par,
The development work had got the wings,
The road, thermal and hydal project station, electricity and dams of irrigation were on strings,
There was no tax for the farmers leads to amount of harvesting that Insteel needed,
Everything was going in the direction that Insteel wanted to had,
But in the meanwhile one of the neighbour of Insteel declared war,

Insteel was not ready for it and had lost the war and a piece of land to the neighbour czar,
The war was painful not because Insteel lost the war poorly,
But because a mask of friend defeated Insteel and not an enemy merely,
The pain of war affected badly the Prime,
After an year or two he died leaving behind a legacy and new Insteel for his successors regime,
The dusk happened when a sun set in the history of Insteel,
But how far it would be darkness, the new dawn was ready and waiting to heal,
The new Prime was appointed to deal with the situation,
He was the new analyzer of the problems faced by Insteel in the fashion,
He arbitrated all the discontinuity of the then condition in a new avatar,
And restored peace, harmony and strength in the farmer's plough and soldier's radar,
Then there was another war was going to be prepared in the destiny of Insteel in its fences,
The second war between Insteel and the parted land from it during the time of independence,
The war was happening due to the piece of land called "Vee",
Vee was the paradise, sober, simplified, full of nature's gift like a bee,
The parted land want Vee from Insteel at any cost,
Often beauty is the degree of top layer of evaluation at most,
The parted land lost the war, like a fire get off by the fire extinguisher,
The Prime was noble man and had decided to negotiate with the counterpart viewer,

The time has another plan for the future of Insteelians that advances,
Soon the second noble Prime departed in an unknown circumstances,
time is an unknown customer, no one knows what it would deal,
Time is a unknown customer , no one knows what it would deal,
The next Prime was ready to hold the power of Insteelian government made of steel,
She was a flexible lady with all the junctions at the right place,
She had made the country full of temperaments of new grace,
There were challenges all togeather in her path,
But her persistance was above and more than any other Prime in the past poitical math,
The new Prime yearning was so difinitive and concurrent with the situation,
That every one knows she would be a rockstar who was born to still every tide's elevation,
She had soon confirmed that she was not for the short time but a long marathon runner,
She ventured all the political tool to magnify the shortcomings and error,
And shorted out it with zeal in her face, and strength in her action,
The leading lady faced many throne in her ways by political disagreement and consequently a part had becme fraction,
But the breakdown did not affected the then Prime,
And she came down heavily on her plitical oppnents every time,
Insteel was facing poverty, unemployment, food crisis and industrial shortages,
With new plans in revolutionary methods she had overcome the food crisis and other challenges smoothly to provide passages,
The war season was not over for Insteel to Grill,

Again the war had ffurther divided the parted coutry by Insteel,
The time was moving fastly, Insteel was also moving furiously,
In collecting arms Insteel was not much far behind from the world norm,
Prime had tested nuclear weapon in the race to enlarge its new role in the world forum,
With great momentum we often move ahead of destiny,
The lady Prime had also done a mistake in the journey,
Or we could say that she had walked ahead of the time to install her overconcerned and moving mistake,
In the quest of concern she overlooked the conition and tried to "manipulate the normalcy"of the country, may be wearing mask,
But she clearly admitted her mistake and rectified it with her equally restrained manner,
She was thoroughly critisized by her opponents, and also withn her cabinet, to stir,
If you see in history some people were not granted forgiveness or the situation did not prevail it,
Same in the case of the leading lady, she lost her life in chasing to pay back the price to manpulate,
Her death causes major unrest and a situation of civil war erupted,
In the eye of the common man, she was a lady ahead of her time and tested,
Things stabilizes time heals everything,
The new Prime was ready to take charge,
The new Prime was young, brave, and adventurist man to recharge,
The Insteel with his innovative ideas, outspoken attitude, and fresh vision to all the problems,
I would call him a simplistic genius who had a new and simple

perspective to all the themes,
He was inexperienced, but that he had taken as the opportunity to start a new era of policy making,
He initiated a reform in economic policies and introduced new working culture with new faces and undertakings,
He specified power to individual to deal with every problem separately with new tools,
And cleared the mess created due to the accessive interferences between the ministers in former rulers,
He introduced new foreign policies, new space program and information technology in the Insteel's vein and arteries,
As he was shining and astonishing in new forms, the other side of coin shows his inability to handle political ease,
He had not effectively managed a neighbour raising ethnic conflict,
Or I can say according to his critics he had overreacted to it,
But I will say he was doing according to his conscience and what he had felt alarming,
He was a leader of exceptions as well as mass, and a character everlasting,
Many time opposition toppled his government,
But the Prime was uneffected of them while fighting and trying to get the majority mandate,
But in the meanwhile the flame from the neighbour country had changed into a self tormenting explosion,
That had took life of the Prime in cruel season,
Or it could be said that an eclipse in the new era of political discourse of Insteel,
With these things were happening there was a parallel conversation and consent in the Vee's politics,

And many native were forced to move from vee to different part of Insteel,
The parted country also started a new war fare terrorizing the Insteel,
And the people of Vee and thus trying to separate it considering it a troubled land,
Side by side a new political group had emerged on the communal line or the right group on the other hand,
This party demolished a building realizing it as a triggered land of one of their deity,
In the beginning it was not a political move, it was actually a condemnation to register against other religion and their Almighty,
But later it could be said that it became a core political agenda to let their religious sentiment live by the new right wing party,
Between all these, the next Prime came into power with people mandate,
The next Prime with his team bring about economic liberalization and infer season of reform to initiate,
Which course corrected the down market policy with socio-economic reforms,
Economy become the most sensitive subject under the new Prime and then economic securedness was not beyond norms,
Then the new independent and accountable Insteel was born to nurture under a new cloud,
Which was hiding the intense heat of sun and also sprinkling water at the time of drought,
The nomadic economic culture came to halt and a stable upgradation was the constant change,
Change should be just, and fade and fume were to exchange,
Old methods dumped , new methods and reforms affirmed,

For new government policy sky was the limit and that was confirmed,
Time passed the new era of coalition government on the cards,
The people of Insteel had choose the change inwards,
A new government came into power but with mixed mandate,
The uncertainty hurted the mandate and more than two or three Prime were changed and rechanged in short dates,
Finally a coalition government came into power to give five year rule to shape Insteel's future,
Economic policies were strengthened under a capable Prime,
Fiscal deficits, debts motioned down under the new regime,
When all these thing were happening the proxy war of terrorizing the environment in Insteel was going on,
Resulted in a more intense clouds of war in the borders of Insteel and parted one;
The war was disastrous, and so disastrous was its aftermath,
Insteel started feeling the heat of price rise and imprudent path,
Season of fresh election restored and this time the old grand party came in power again,
One of the hero of liberalization of economy in Insteel was become consensus based Prime man,
He started a new chapter of growth then became an old irony,
There were historic deal happened in the tenure of this Prime,
Like nuclear deals given wings to the old birds flying in the rhyme,
The super success of first term assured the second term for grand old party,
Insteel journey to become self reliant country had become reality,
The sufficiency in food reserve, success in telecom sector to space invasion,
India became a peaceful and harmonious nation,

Along with this the neighbour parted country couldn't see Insteel's happiness,
While supporting its proxy war of terror outfit it attacked a city a Insteel created stress,
Insteel assured retaliation strongly, terrorists either gunned down or faced trial,
During all these one of the major achievement of this government was it isolated the parted country and it's terrors outfit for a while,
This govt also had contradicted in various scam,
And for a short time opposition became succesful in proving the government is tainted and in corruption frame,
This caused outburst in people, pertaining havoc and leaded to suspension of the govt. in the election,
Even though later all the charges that were framed remained false and needed correction,
The coalition era finished with the massive majority to a single large party or to the right wing;
The new Prime assumed the office he was enjoying his office and massive swing,
New schemes were lounched regarding cleanliness drive, new production hub and smooth economic feeds,
But there was a doubt from opposition citing difference in words and deeds,
I must say, economy was fine but a big blunder was committed in the form of demonetization,
The insensitive move hurting to the medium and poor class in the fascination,
But the foundation of Insteel by then was very strong and can resist such blows,

Even though the govt. did another error by hastily implemented GST in the stream flow,

Causing instability but I must say this govt. had courage to take big steps,

Which it needed to take in suited direction and shapes,

Reform are not done in a day, it comes by partial perfection and it's reasonable displays,

As long as one sticks to basic discipline to run the nation it would help back and relays,

An extreme path in economic, socio-economic , social structure was never meant for mild Insteel,

Insteel was never in a short run it had to cover the longest run in world to deal,

Insteel was great, it had been greater, and it was born to be greatest, that I do feel.

32. TRANSFIGURED

There was an old tree,
Where two sparrow were living,
In their nest, & free,
Without any problem & with feeling;

Also there were five butterflies,
Living near the sparrows nest,
The butterflies had a habit,
To criticize sparrow and imitate;

The butterflies used to make fun,
Of the sparrows unitedly,
There sparrows were calm& know turn,
That the butterflies, alike secretly;

One day when the sparrows were not in their nest,
The butterflies came & occupy the nest
And started playing in the nest happily in fest,
There colored wing yellow and black were shining in haste;

Suddenly the sparrows came back,
& the butterflies had to fly away,
Who was greater & who was really imitating in the wake?
Or were they familiarizing and equilibrium in the way?

33. What Can Exist?

Nothing go waste,
Whatever we think,
Are the shadows of ourselves,
But the shadow can be thin in sufferings,
And dark in joy,
Moreover,the fringes vary,
In accordance with the limelight of character,
These character fringes are the will:
Which can climb mountain,
Can cross the sea,
Or even can prevail destiny to change,
But then comes exceptions;
Hallucination: where mind dwells,
Without any wings,
Wasted thinking, and untruth,
Unfollowing the rules,
where even the nil;
Is not even a empty rhetoric,
A non existential dwelling.

Printed by Libri Plureos GmbH in Hamburg,
Germany

9 798888 151174